KEEP GOING MOMO

The millipede who dreamed big 

BHANI JALKRISH

Illustrator

JAYALAKSHMI GOPALAKRISHNAN

Made with ♥ on the Notion Press Platform
www.notionpress.com

Thank you to my family, friends, and all my well-wishers
for your love and support.

This book is dedicated to
my two little spudlets — Buu and Gungee.

Meet Momo, the baby millipede.

With ten little feet, no bigger than a seed.

She had a goal, mighty and tall.

She wanted to be the longest of them all.

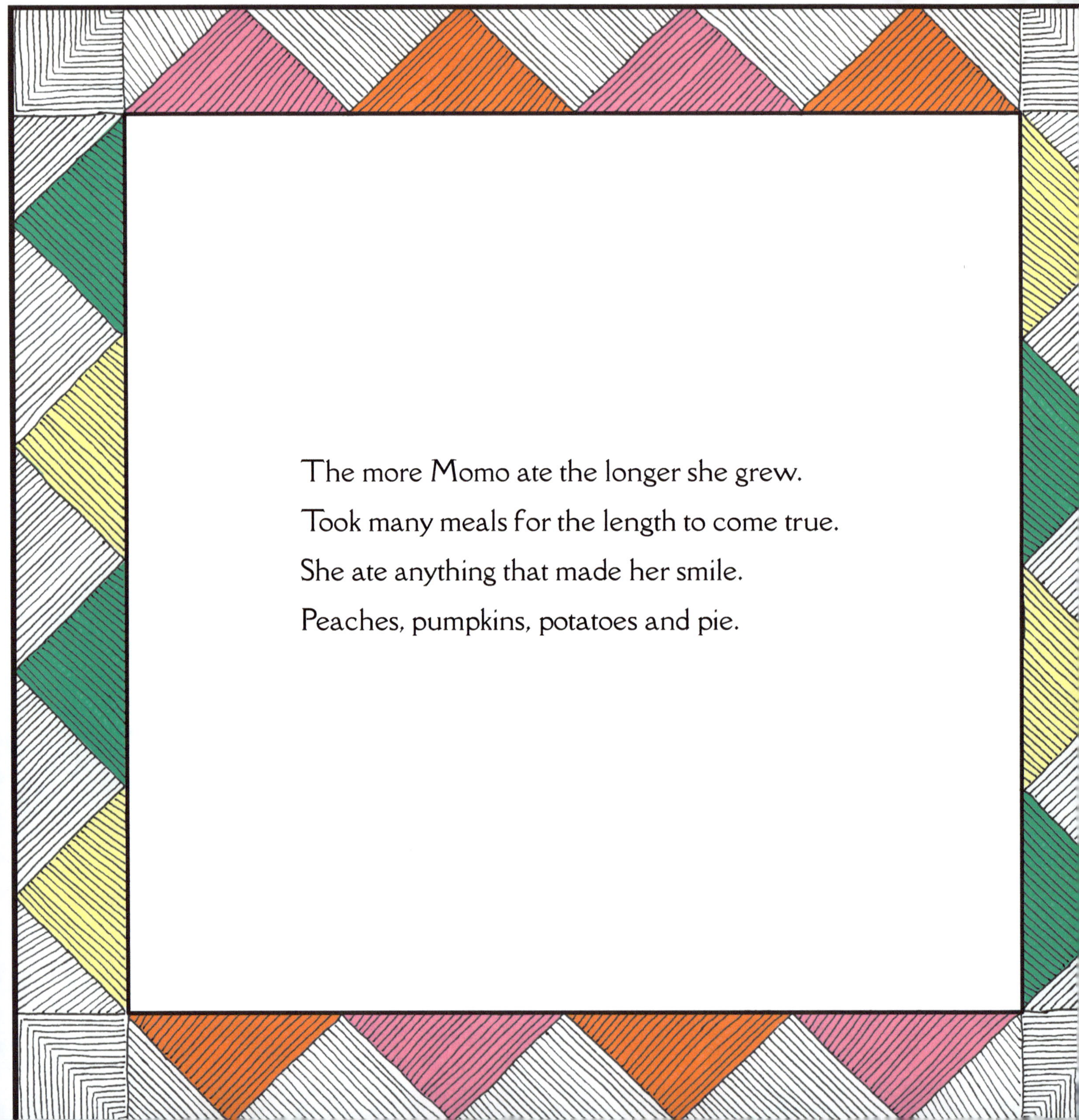

The more Momo ate the longer she grew.

Took many meals for the length to come true.

She ate anything that made her smile.

Peaches, pumpkins, potatoes and pie.

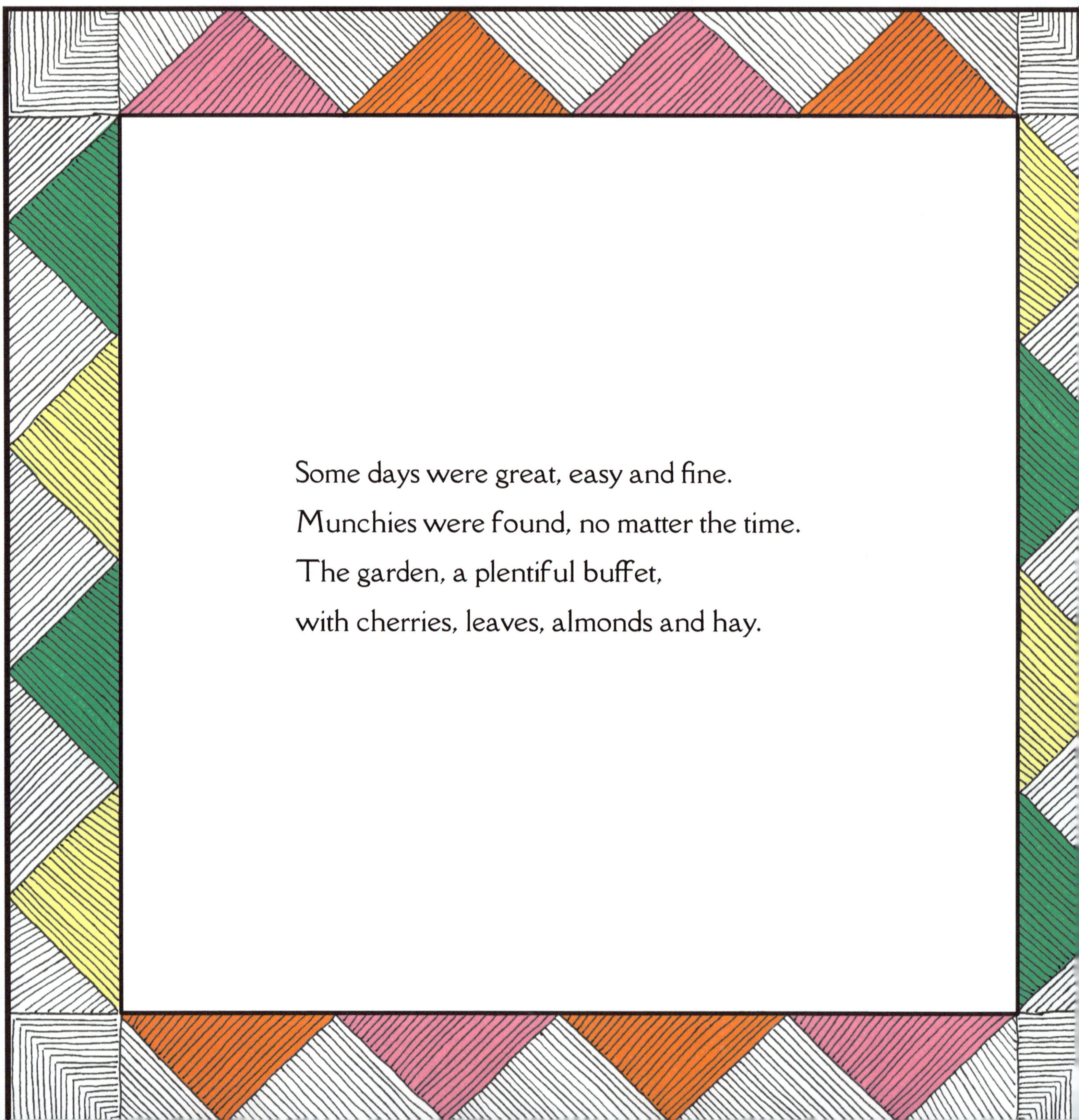

Some days were great, easy and fine.

Munchies were found, no matter the time.

The garden, a plentiful buffet,

with cherries, leaves, almonds and hay.

Some days were dull, difficult, and hard.

Barely any food in the entire yard.

Not even the odd pit, seed or rind.

Even motivation was hard to find.

Some days were fun, jolly and happy,
as little Momo's friends came in handy.
Buu, the butterfly and Gungee, the bee,
were giving away some sweet honey.

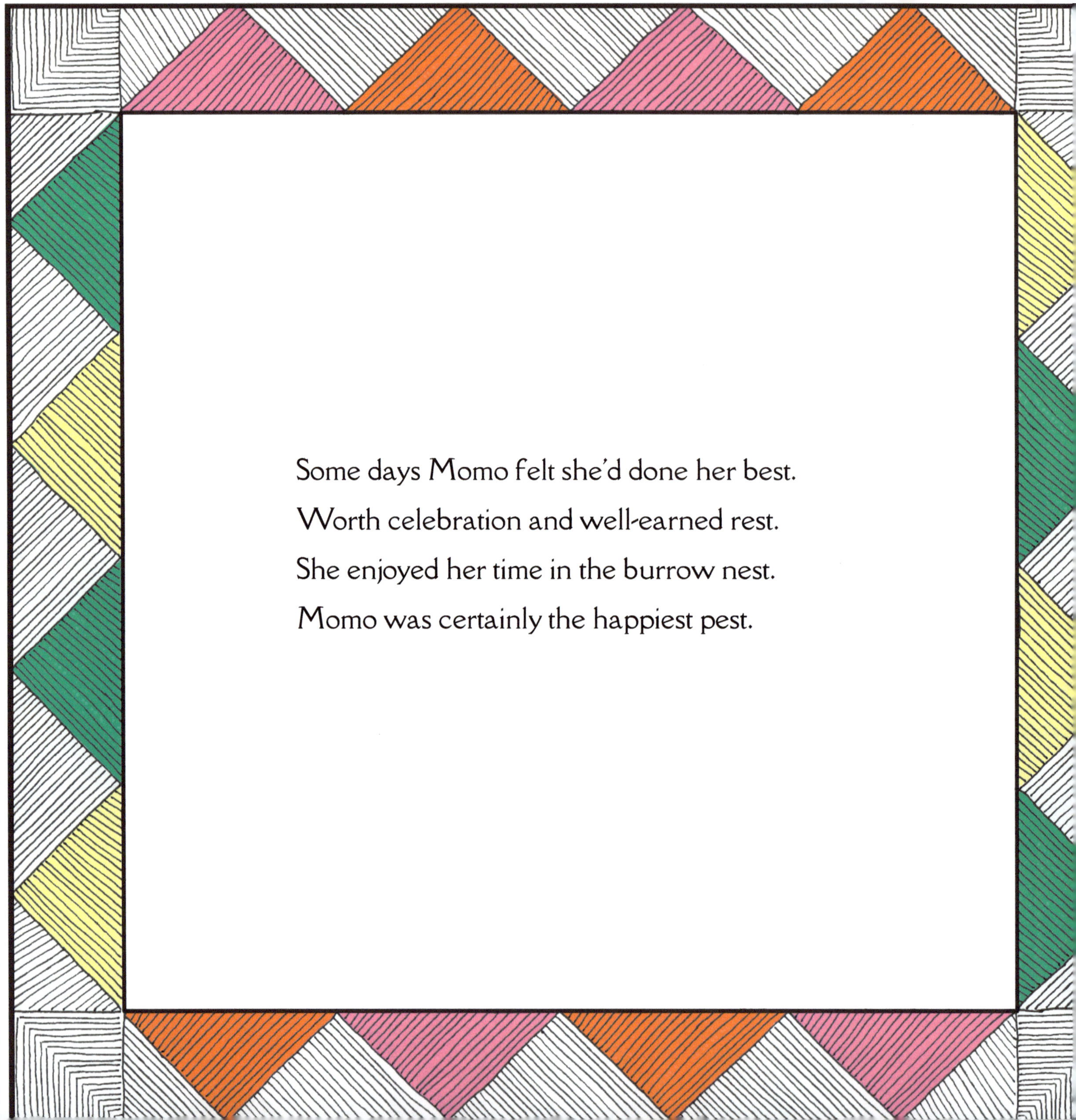

Some days Momo felt she'd done her best.

Worth celebration and well-earned rest.

She enjoyed her time in the burrow nest.

Momo was certainly the happiest pest.

Momo never rushed or made haste.

She moved forward at her own steady pace.

Unbothered by the hiccups on the way.

She knew every nibble would add up one day.

All the insects cheered on Momo's feat.

Her personal best, she now had reached.

Was it sixty, eighty, or hundred feet?
Gungee and Buu lost count indeed.

Keep going Momo, you amazing millipede!
You should be proud of what you achieved.